Sion

Bianca Roberts

Presentation by *BookLeaf Publishing*

Web: www.bookleafpub.com

E-mail: info@bookleafpub.com

ISBN: 9789358317800

First edition 2023

ACKNOWLEDGEMENT

Thank you to my family and friends who inspire and support me. I love you all.

The First Bite

I have been waiting all day.
It feels like so much more.
I'm starving.
As the saliva begins to pour.
Like water flowing downstream
The urgency sets in, as I take a deep breath,
Waiting for it to come
I wipe my mouth as I sit in excitement
Ready to enjoy every single crumb.
The steam circles around the plate.

Here it comes…

It's delicious.

Caged

I lay here, pounding at the walls.
Yelling, wondering if someone will help me if
they fall.
Then, I sit down, look around, and stare.
To witness the beauty of it all.
The grooves of the chain fences dance as I
knock on them.
Softly, softer, then not at all.
The warden comes in
He throws the key on the floor.
But I didn't even see it
I only wanted to lay here a little bit longer
With the walls that I adore.

A Journey That Never Happened

Three hikers decide to take a road trip.
They pack their bags filled to the brim.
With everything they own, but the clothes they
are in.

Day and night
They travel the world and see captivating sights,

Day and night
They look outside and wonder what they should
do tonight.

Then I wake up.
I hear the door open.
And they say, "Are you ready?"

We Come and Go

The revolving door shakes as its tested once
again by the endless people that push through,
With no care in the world of the weight it feels
And how long it has felt used.
Each repeated use like an earthquake,
A force bigger than any one person could
imagine or anticipate.
One by one they dissipate.
Until there is none left.
Because this is its job.
With every touch, it says hello and goodbye.
To the possibilities.
To what could have been.
And what is.

It's Just That Simple

Today is a wonderful day.
I walked outside and saw the most beautiful
bird.
Enjoying the rain as it drank from the puddles on
the ground undeterred.
Then I heard a guitar player playing the most
beautiful sound I've ever heard.
I went to dinner and ate the most flavorful meal
I've ever had.
Then I had the most sound sleep that made me
question if anything in my life has ever gone
bad.
Today is a wonderful day.
Isn't it?
And I am sure all the others will be too.

Or is it?

Today is a wonderful…
No, I don't think so.
I walked outside and saw the colors drain out of
the sky as a storm began forming in front of my
eyes.
Then I heard the most off-putting sound I've
ever heard, as a person attempted to play the
guitar.
He undoubtedly failed.
To lighten the mood, I went to dinner and the
service was appalling.
As I struggled to sleep it off, I could not stop
myself from bawling.
Today is a terrible day.
Isn't it?
And I am sure all the others will be too.

Quiet Time

Shhh…
Be quiet.
She can hear your footsteps
Your deep breaths
Your whispers being carried along the halls with heft
The bookshelves bereft, of color,
As you beg for another,
Minute, to enjoy
The silence that this room deploys
Like a bomb being dropped in the air
Meant to annoy,
Those hanging,
To ensure they recognize and respect the clanging,
Of the books against the scanner
Writing in your newly bought planner
Waiting to be filled with ideas in any manner.
With the new knowledge you just acquired
I hope you become everything, you desired.

A Murder Mystery

A detective walks in.
The room ripe with sin.
Looking with his magnifying glass.
Who the killer might have been.
The woman with no care walking into the night.
The man who obviously has been looking for a
fight.
The old lady who looks like she might be the
next one dead filled with fright.
"Alright", the detective says, "I think I know
who it is."
The blood trail curves,
And swerves,
And leads him towards the killer.
So he thinks.
But all he sees.
Is a mirror.
"Does this mean…?", he wonders.
Until the lights turn off.
The mirror breaks,
The room shakes.
And he feels a vicious thump.
It looks like…
There's been another murder.
And so…
A detective walks in.

The Darkened Medal

Side by side
The plaques,
The trophies,
The medals, sit on the wall.
As she remembers the journey.
Before it all came to a crawl.
She hears the bones snapping.
On repeat
The mask she wore for the last time fully
cracking.
A person she could never beat.
Her win taken by the jaws of what she knew was
an inevitable defeat.
She sighs in relief.
Here it is.
Collecting dust.
A gust of wind blows the closet door closed.
Never to be seen again.

Trial by Fire

The burning smell spreads.
It tickles the noses of everyone in the room.
"It's a fire", they all say.
"I'm sure it will be taken care of."
"Someday."
Then, everyone heads back to their beds.

A Burning Question

Oh no!
Quick!
The oracle is here!
What should I ask?
Should I talk about all the things,
That'll never come to past?!
Or the stuff that will or will not last?!
Or if my life, fragile and made of glass
Will shatter, once first harassed?!
At the first sign of trouble that will leave a gash
No!
That question might be a little bit too crass.
There's no way that question is worth being
asked.
Oh…
Wait.
Never mind.
He already left.
Phew.
Maybe next time.

A familiar voice

Good morning,
i hear you say.
i love you.
words that will never go away.
i can smell the coffee brewing.
i can hear you in the shower.
and I know you'll be gone in less than an hour.
i feel a soft kiss on my cheek.
it looks like we're out of time,
i can barely speak.
but I don't have to.
your voice says enough for the both of us.
your voice says more than I ever could.

Intruder

Seeds drop to the ground.
Hoping to be brought to life.
It looks like flowers are in season.
And they survived,
Despite the strife.
The bitter winter,
The sweltering sun.
Until it all became undone
The leaves wither and drop,
Continuing every day.
Nonstop.
As the flowers were on their last breath.
A stranger passed by.
The sweat off the stranger's brow dripped onto
the flowers.
An entirely new supply.
Reviving the once dead leaves.
The stranger walked on.
The flowers could once again enjoy the cool
breeze.
As the flowers called for him to make it known
what he had done.
It seemed to be too late.
The stranger had disappeared.

Dinner Table

Steak is sizzling.
Rice is steaming.
Soup is simmering.
The timer is set.
Let's take a break for game night.
Three more minutes
We sit down waiting,
Debating who is going to start,
Or part with a token or two
Delighted, excited, angry thinking about who is
going to lose,
Two more minutes
Game after game
Looking for someone to blame
Laughing it off until we start again
One more minute
A battle of wits coming to pass
Back and forth
Someone is in last
Until someone unexpectedly surpassed,
The one in first
Who could it be?
Right at the end
There are no guarantees
It looks like…
Ding! Ding! Ding!
Dinner is served.

Uphill Battle

Swords sing as they clash
Arrows fly making a splash, where they land.
The general and his soldiers sprint through the ashes
Ignoring their bodies riddled with scratches.
The debris falls upon them
Sisyphus would be proud
The soldiers never noticed
Not at all through the cloud.
After everything.
They barely moved an inch.

Fly

Shooting stars blaze in the sky
One wish
It's coming soon.
It was promised.
Has everything changed?
Has anything changed at all?
It has.
I can feel it.

Try Again

Hands trembling
As I stack the tower
It crumbles
Right in front of me
It has fallen apart
Try again.

The brush scrapes against the easel
The teacher scoffs at the disappointing image in
front of her
Nearly surprised such a drawing isn't illegal
The canvas rips in half
Try again.

The numbers ring inside my head
What did he just say
The cash is here and it's my first day
I'll just hand him the money
One, two, three, four
Wait
I think I've been robbed
Try again.

Snip, snip, snip
Strands of hair float onto the floor
Distracted, I realize that might be one too many
There is not a strand of hair left on her head
Try again.

I delegate with precision,
I don't have to ask for permission,
Everything is my decision,
I think I found it.
Perfection.

Grown

Locked in place.
Stuck in time.
Day after day.
The endless grind.
I look in the mirror and cannot recognize
I think I witnessed my own demise
And its strange because I cannot surmise
What happened to cause this disguise,
That I embrace,
To become such a disgrace
Its something I need to erase
Luckily, its never too late to deface
The one who is standing there.
There is no need to compare
There is plenty of time to repair
Because I declare, war, on despair
And I am prepared, to fight.

A Simmering Mind

The chemistry
The grooves
That are oh so refined

Pulses,
Coming in and out of your mind,
It is what makes you so defined
A mad scientist wonders why it's so divine

A scientific anomaly

A marvel

The eighth wonder of the world right in front of
his eyes

He picks up the scalpel
Ready to make the discovery of a lifetime

Encore

My first live performance.
It went so well.
I never believed I would truly excel
Now I need something to dispel, all these fears,
As they cheer my name begging for more,
This is more than I bargained for.
Will I leave them wanting or go back out and
give them an encore
Before they all forget my name, and I no longer
soar

The Last Bite

The pangs of hunger that once shook me to my
core have vanished.
I am no longer famished.
But it seems like dessert is still coming.
Last call.
I need to finish off this meal.
Don't leave a single morsel left.
Before it's over.
I take a deep breath,
Waiting for it come
The fountain dripping from my mouth has run
dry.
It's time to say goodbye.

Here it comes…

It's delicious.